DEFINING MOMENTS IN CANADIAN HISTORY

Bringing Home
THE CONSTITUTION

LESTER B. PEARSON H.S.
LIBRARY

Weigl

Published by Weigl Educational Publishers Limited
6325 10th Street SE
Calgary, Alberta, Canada T2H 2Z9
Website: www.weigl.ca

Copyright ©2012 WEIGL EDUCATIONAL PUBLISHERS LIMITED
All rights reserved. No part of this publication may be reproduced, stored in a retrieval system, or transmitted in any form or by any means, electronic, mechanical, photocopying, recording, or otherwise, without the prior written permission of the publisher.

All of the Internet URLs given in the book were valid at the time of publication. However, due to the dynamic nature of the Internet, some addresses may have changed, or sites may have ceased to exist since publication. While the author and publisher regret any inconvenience this may cause readers, no responsibility for any such changes can be accepted by either the author or the publisher.

Library and Archives Canada Cataloguing-in-Publication Data available upon request.
Fax (403) 233-7769 for the attention of the Publishing Records department.

ISBN 978-1-77071-686-5

Printed in the United States of America in North Mankato, Minnesota
1 2 3 4 5 6 7 8 9 0   15 14 13 12 11

072011
WEP040711

Senior Editor: Heather Kissock
Art Director: Terry Paulhus

Every reasonable effort has been made to trace ownership and to obtain permission to reprint copyright material.

The publishers would be pleased to have any errors or omissions brought to their attention so that they may be corrected in subsequent printings.

We acknowledge the financial support of the Government of Canada through the Canada Book Fund for our publishing activities.

Contents

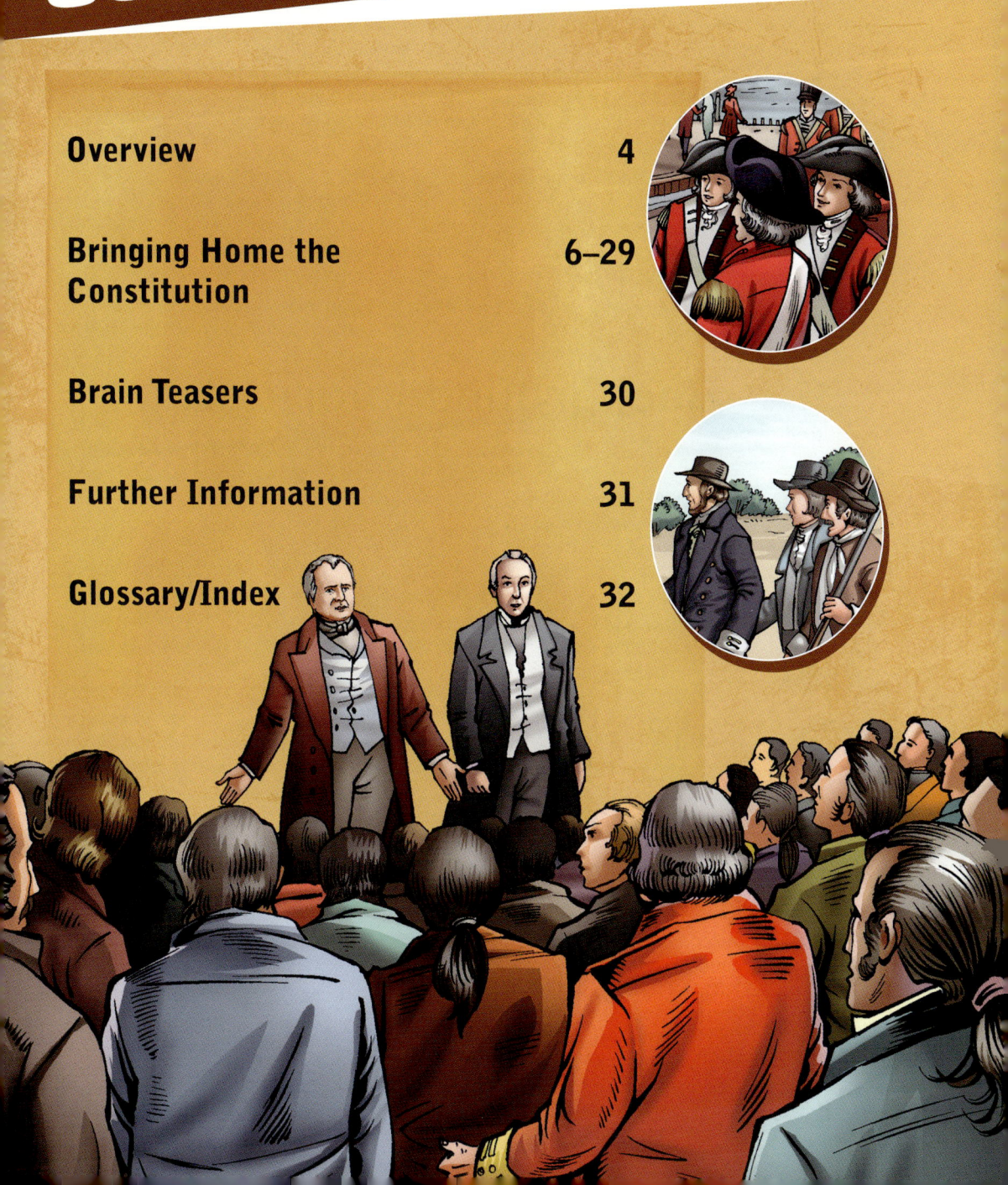

Overview — 4

Bringing Home the Constitution — 6–29

Brain Teasers — 30

Further Information — 31

Glossary/Index — 32

Overview

Canada's parliamentary **democracy** grew out of its colonial European roots. The first Europeans, Norse traders, visited Canada's shores in the ninth century. Hundreds of years would pass before the country and the current form of government took shape. Until the 17th century, Aboriginal Peoples thrived across North America. Following visits by European explorers like John Cabot, Jacques Cartier, Samuel de Champlain, and Henry Hudson, the French established a permanent colony known as New France. This colony stretched from Newfoundland to the Great Lakes region. Meanwhile, to the south, 13 American colonies had been established.

For years, Great Britain and France competed for control of the land and resources in North America as well as for power in Europe. Then, in 1756, the Seven Years War, known as the French and Indian War in the colonies, erupted. At its conclusion, France ceded all of its American colonies east of the Mississippi River to Great Britain. The British government now ruled in New France, but soon, its governance would be challenged.

Out of the colonies would emerge two new nations, the Dominion of Canada and the United States of America. They would not be ruled by the British Parliament. Instead, they would be governed by their own peoples and their own constitutions.

Background Information

Guy Carleton – Guy Carleton served as governor of Quebec from 1768 to 1778 and again from 1785 to 1795. His attempts to reconcile the French colonial elite to British rule led to passage of the Quebec Act in 1774. He later became known as Lord Dorchester, after being appointed Baron of Dorchester.

William Wyndham Grenville – William Grenville, known as Lord Grenville, served much of his life in the British Parliament. In 1791, as leader of the House of Lords, Lord Grenville authored the Constitution Act, which would govern Lower and Upper Canada.

Elijah Harper – Elijah Harper served as a provincial legislator for Manitoba, as Minister for Northern Affairs, and as Minister Responsible for Native Affairs. From 1987 through 1990, he led the effort to defeat the **Meech Lake Accord**, which failed to secure adequate recognition or self-government for Aboriginal peoples.

John George Lambton – John Lambton, known as Lord Durham, served as governor general of Canada from 1838 to 1839. In 1839, he published his *Report on the Affairs of British North America*. This document, commonly called the Durham Report, proposed the union of Lower and Upper Canada under a more representative government.

Pierre Elliott Trudeau – Pierre Trudeau served as prime minister of Canada from 1968 to 1979 and from 1980 to 1984. As prime minister, he led the effort for constitutional reform. In 1982, he succeeded in winning passage of a new Constitution Act, which achieved Canadian independence from the British Parliament.

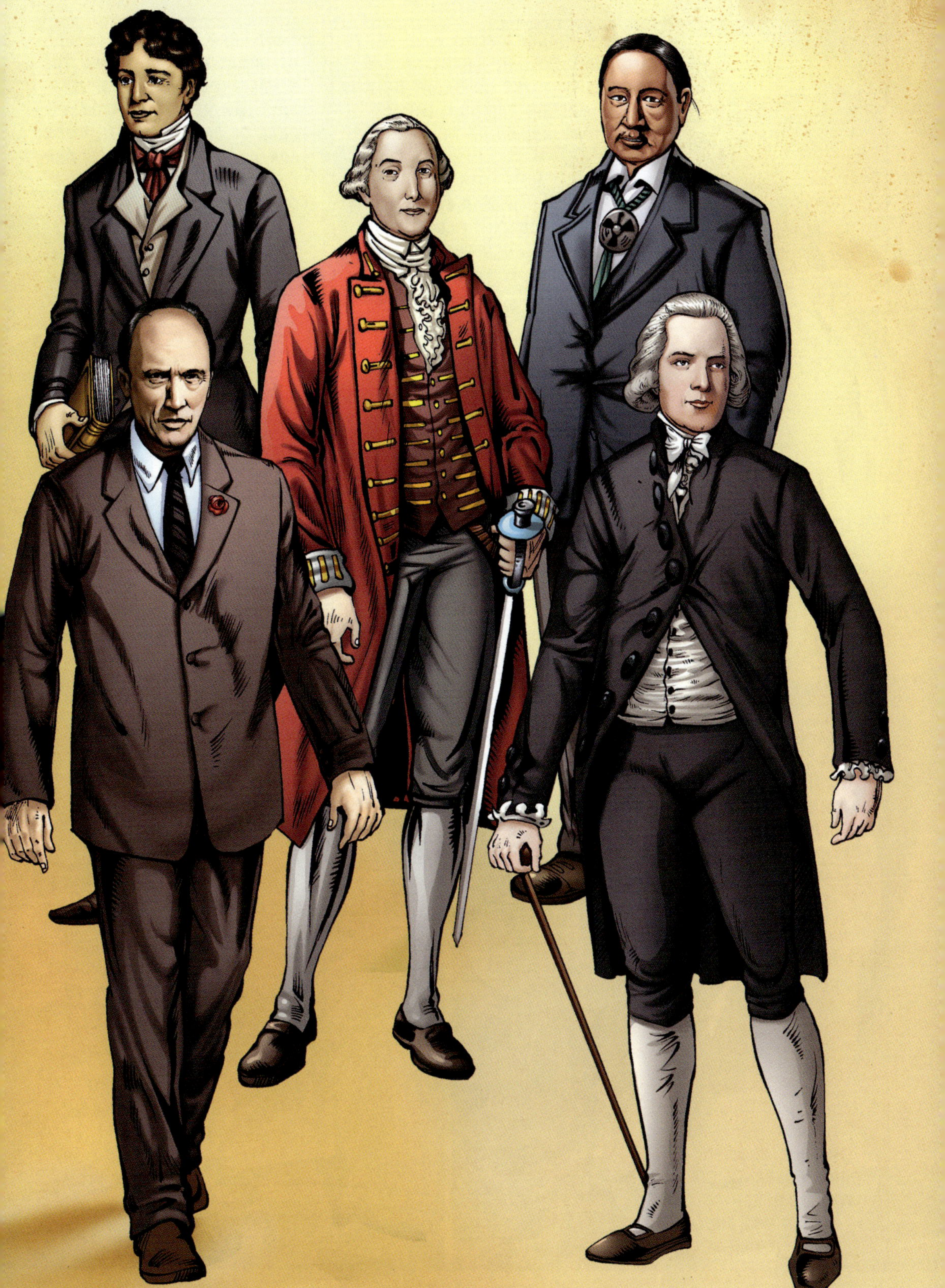

IN 1763, FRANCE CEDED RULE OF ITS AMERICAN COLONIES EAST OF THE MISSISSIPPI RIVER TO GREAT BRITAIN. GREAT BRITAIN GAINED A LARGE TERRITORY KNOWN AS NEW FRANCE.
THE SEVEN YEARS WAR IS OVER. YOU HAVE LOST.
YES, BUT IT IS A FRENCH COLONY, FILLED WITH FRENCH PEOPLE, THAT YOU HAVE WON.
Lake Huron
Lake Michigan
NEW FRANCE
ATLANTIC OCEAN
THAT YEAR, KING GEORGE III OF GREAT BRITAIN ISSUED THE ROYAL PROCLAMATION OF 1763. THIS LAW RESERVED A GREAT DEAL OF LAND IN NORTH AMERICA FOR ABORIGINAL PEOPLES, AND IT ESTABLISHED THE COLONY OF QUEBEC.
NEW FRANCE IS NO MORE. QUEBEC SHALL BE GOVERNED BY A BRITISH GOVERNOR WITH THE POWER TO CALL AN ASSEMBLY.
UNLIKE THE PROTESTANT BRITISH, FRENCH COLONISTS WERE ROMAN CATHOLIC. BRITISH LAW PROHIBITED ROMAN CATHOLICS FROM SERVING IN GOVERNMENT AND FROM VOTING. THIS TRADITION CREATED PROBLEMS FOR QUEBEC'S FIRST GOVERNOR, GENERAL JAMES MURRAY.
MOST OF THE PEOPLE IN YOUR COLONY CANNOT VOTE. THEY CANNOT SERVE IN GOVERNMENT.
WE NEED TO **ASSIMILATE** THE FRENCH. THEY WILL HAVE TO ADOPT OUR WAYS.
WE CANNOT MAKE THE FRENCH BECOME ENGLISH, AND I CAN'T GOVERN A COLONY OF 70,000 FRENCH COLONISTS WITH 500 ENGLISH COLONISTS.
AS GOVERNOR, GENERAL MURRAY RESISTED CALLS TO ASSIMILATE THE FRENCH. HE ALLOWED THE FRENCH TO SERVE IN GOVERNMENT AND TO HELP HIM MAKE LAWS.
DID YOU HEAR WHAT HE'S DONE NOW? THE GOVERNOR HAS CREATED FRENCH COURTS.
FRENCH LAWS IN AN ENGLISH COLONY—IT'S TRAITOROUS!
HE IS REFUSING TO CALL AN ASSEMBLY. WE HAVE RIGHTS, TOO.

BRITISH DISCONTENT WITH GENERAL MURRAY'S POLICIES LED TO HIS RECALL. IN 1766, GENERAL MURRAY RETURNED TO ENGLAND TO STAND TRIAL. ALTHOUGH HE WAS ACQUITTED, MURRAY DID NOT RETURN TO QUEBEC.

I SECURED A COLONY FULL OF FRENCH SETTLERS FOR THE BRITISH AS BEST I COULD.

IN 1768, SIR GUY CARLETON REPLACED GENERAL MURRAY AS GOVERNOR OF QUEBEC. HE BEGAN BY ELIMINATING FRENCH COUNCIL MEMBERS.

I WILL NOT MAKE THE SAME MISTAKES AS MURRAY.

GOVERNOR CARLETON SOON LEARNED THAT RULING THE FRENCH PEOPLE OF QUEBEC WAS NOT SO SIMPLE. LIKE GENERAL MURRAY, HE REFUSED TO HOLD ELECTIONS WHEN ONLY A SMALL NUMBER OF ENGLISH COLONISTS COULD PARTICIPATE.

WHAT CAN I DO? THIS LAND MUST BE RULED BY ITS PEOPLE, AND ITS PEOPLE ARE FRENCH.

BRITISH MERCHANTS COMPLAINED ABOUT CARLETON AS THEY HAD ABOUT GENERAL MURRAY, BUT CARLETON APPEALED TO THE BRITISH PARLIAMENT TO WORK WITH THE FRENCH ELITE OF QUEBEC.

THE 13 AMERICAN COLONIES MAY REVOLT SOON. WE NEED THE FRENCH OF QUEBEC ON OUR SIDE. TO WIN THEIR SUPPORT, I HAVE ALLOWED THEM TO KEEP THEIR LAWS AND CUSTOMS.

GOVERNOR CARLETON TRAVELLED TO ENGLAND AND PRESSED LORD FREDERICK NORTH, THE PRIME MINISTER, TO PASS THE QUEBEC ACT OF 1774.
SO QUEBEC WILL HAVE FRENCH **CIVIL LAW** BUT BRITISH **CRIMINAL LAW**? IN ADDITION, THERE WILL BE NO ELECTED ASSEMBLY, CORRECT?
YES, AND THE FRENCH MUST HAVE FREEDOM OF RELIGION, THEIR LANGUAGE, AND THEIR OLD LANDHOLDING SYSTEM. THERE WILL BE NO ELECTED ASSEMBLY. THE GOVERNOR WILL RULE WITH AN APPOINTED COUNCIL.

THE QUEBEC ACT APPEASED FRENCH CLERGY AND LANDOWNERS, CALLED SEIGNEURS, BUT ANGERED MANY OTHER PEOPLE.
AT LEAST WE HAVE A PLACE FROM WHICH TO LAUNCH BRITISH TROOPS IF THE 13 COLONIES REBEL.

WE ARE RULED BY THE SAME FRENCH PRIESTS AND LANDLORDS AS BEFORE.
WE MUST STILL GIVE WHAT LITTLE MONEY WE HAVE TO THE CHURCH IN DUES.
MY HUSBAND SAYS THE LANDHOLDING SYSTEM IS AS UNFAIR AND AS FEUDAL AS EVER.

THE 13 AMERICAN COLONIES TO THE SOUTH TOOK THE QUEBEC ACT AS FURTHER JUSTIFICATION FOR REVOLUTION.
THE NEW ENGLAND COURANT
The Virginia Gazette
A French Roman Catholic is considered a better subject than a New England Protestant.

IN 1775, WAR BROKE OUT BETWEEN GREAT BRITAIN AND THE PATRIOTS OF THE 13 AMERICAN COLONIES, WHICH DECLARED INDEPENDENCE THE FOLLOWING YEAR. THE AMERICAN REVOLUTION LASTED EIGHT YEARS. IT ENDED IN BRITISH DEFEAT.

IN 1783, BRITAIN FORMALLY RECOGNIZED THE UNITED STATES AS AN INDEPENDENT NATION.

WE WILL BE PUNISHED FOR BEING BRITISH.

OUR ANCESTORS SETTLED THIS COUNTRY, BUT WE ARE NO LONGER WELCOME HERE.

AFTER THE AMERICAN REVOLUTION, ABOUT 40,000 BRITISH **LOYALISTS** LEFT THE UNITED STATES FOR QUEBEC AND NOVA SCOTIA. THEIR MIGRATION LED TO THE ESTABLISHMENT OF A NEW COLONY, NEW BRUNSWICK.

WE CANNOT STAY IN THE NEW AMERICAN NATION. WE ARE BRITISH SUBJECTS.

WELCOME! THIS LAND, HOWEVER, IS AS FRENCH AS IT IS BRITISH.

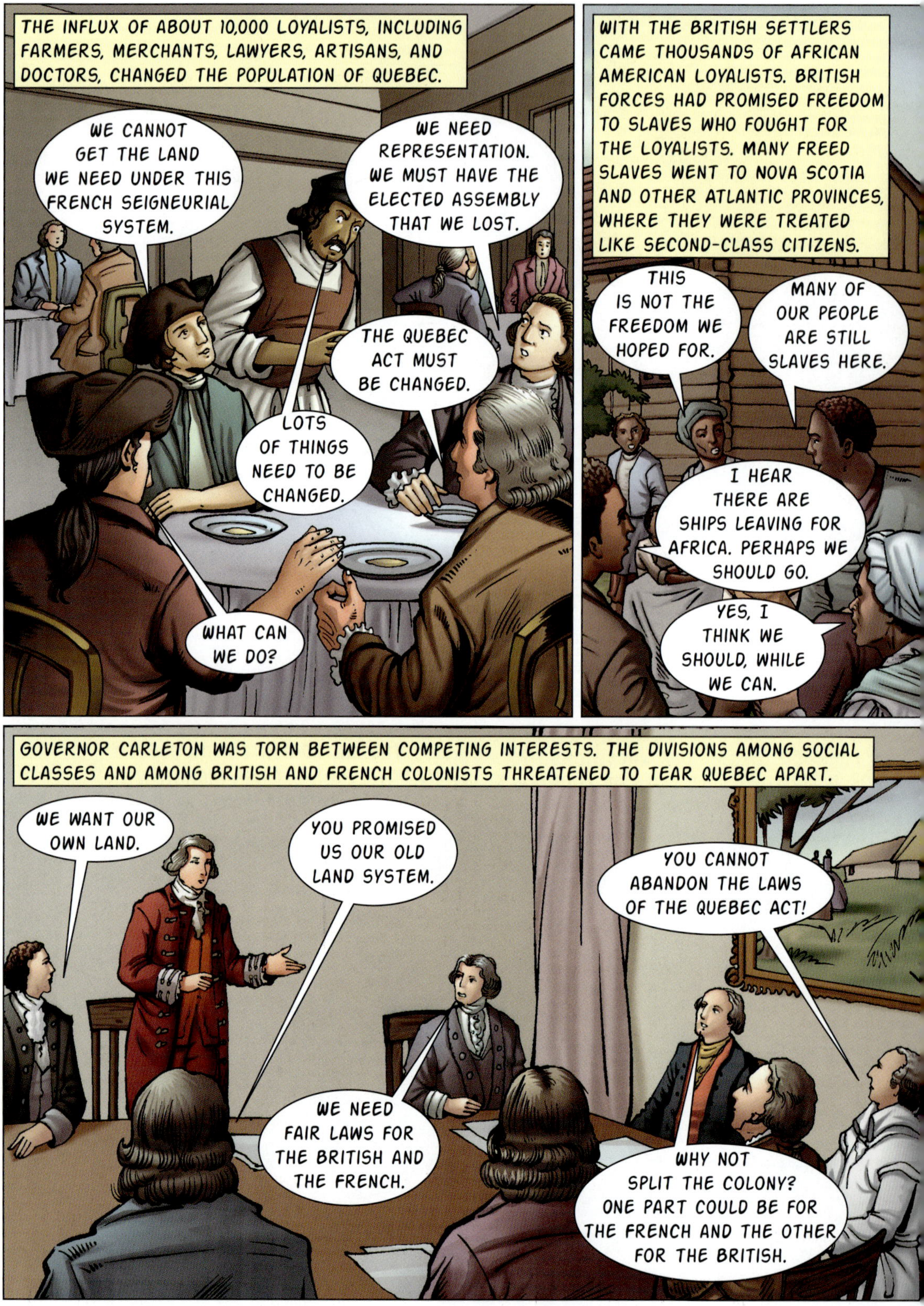
THE INFLUX OF ABOUT 10,000 LOYALISTS, INCLUDING FARMERS, MERCHANTS, LAWYERS, ARTISANS, AND DOCTORS, CHANGED THE POPULATION OF QUEBEC.
WE CANNOT GET THE LAND WE NEED UNDER THIS FRENCH SEIGNEURIAL SYSTEM.
WE NEED REPRESENTATION. WE MUST HAVE THE ELECTED ASSEMBLY THAT WE LOST.
THE QUEBEC ACT MUST BE CHANGED.
LOTS OF THINGS NEED TO BE CHANGED.
WHAT CAN WE DO?
WITH THE BRITISH SETTLERS CAME THOUSANDS OF AFRICAN AMERICAN LOYALISTS. BRITISH FORCES HAD PROMISED FREEDOM TO SLAVES WHO FOUGHT FOR THE LOYALISTS. MANY FREED SLAVES WENT TO NOVA SCOTIA AND OTHER ATLANTIC PROVINCES, WHERE THEY WERE TREATED LIKE SECOND-CLASS CITIZENS.
THIS IS NOT THE FREEDOM WE HOPED FOR.
MANY OF OUR PEOPLE ARE STILL SLAVES HERE.
I HEAR THERE ARE SHIPS LEAVING FOR AFRICA. PERHAPS WE SHOULD GO.
YES, I THINK WE SHOULD, WHILE WE CAN.
GOVERNOR CARLETON WAS TORN BETWEEN COMPETING INTERESTS. THE DIVISIONS AMONG SOCIAL CLASSES AND AMONG BRITISH AND FRENCH COLONISTS THREATENED TO TEAR QUEBEC APART.
WE WANT OUR OWN LAND.
YOU PROMISED US OUR OLD LAND SYSTEM.
YOU CANNOT ABANDON THE LAWS OF THE QUEBEC ACT!
WE NEED FAIR LAWS FOR THE BRITISH AND THE FRENCH.
WHY NOT SPLIT THE COLONY? ONE PART COULD BE FOR THE FRENCH AND THE OTHER FOR THE BRITISH.

THE DEBATE IN QUEBEC LED TO DEBATE IN PARLIAMENT. IN 1791, LORD WILLIAM WYNDHAM GRENVILLE AUTHORED THE CONSTITUTION ACT, WHICH PROPOSED SPLITTING QUEBEC INTO TWO PROVINCES.

THE FRENCH CAN HAVE THEIR WAYS IN LOWER CANADA. THE BRITISH CAN HAVE THEIRS IN UPPER CANADA.

BUT HOW WILL WE GOVERN TWO QUEBECS?

WE WILL GOVERN WITH A GOVERNOR, AN EXECUTIVE AND A LEGISLATIVE COUNCIL, AND AN ELECTED ASSEMBLY.

AT THE SAME TIME, REVOLUTION HAD ERUPTED IN FRANCE. FOLLOWING SO CLOSELY ON THE AMERICAN REVOLUTION, THE VIOLENCE FRIGHTENED BRITISH LEADERS.

A FIERCE DEBATE, LED BY CHARLES JAMES FOX AND EDMUND BURKE, RAGED IN PARLIAMENT. FORMERLY FRIENDS, THE TWO POLITICIANS WERE BITTERLY DIVIDED OVER THE ISSUES OF DEMOCRACY, REVOLUTION, AND GOVERNMENT POWER.
OUR PRESENT DANGER IS FROM ANARCHY—PLUNDERING, FEROCIOUS, BLOODY, TYRANNICAL DEMOCRACY.
WE CANNOT ALLOW THIS VIOLENCE TO REACH QUEBEC!
THE COLONY IS FULLY CAPABLE OF ENJOYING POLITICAL FREEDOM.
TO PREVENT REVOLUTION, WE MUST GRANT ITS PEOPLE THE SAME FREEDOMS AS THE AMERICANS HAVE, LEST THEY LOOK ON THEIR NEIGHBORS WITH ENVY!
FOX'S VIEWS FAILED TO SWAY BURKE, GRENVILLE, PRIME MINISTER WILLIAM PITT, OR A MAJORITY OF PARLIAMENT.
PRIME MINISTER, WE MUST HAVE **REPRESENTATIVE DEMOCRACY** AND PROVIDE A **RESPONSIBLE GOVERNMENT**, WITHOUT GIVING INTO EXCESSIVE DEMANDS BY ANY GROUP.
I AGREE. FOX GOES TOO FAR. WE MUST DIVIDE AND RULE.

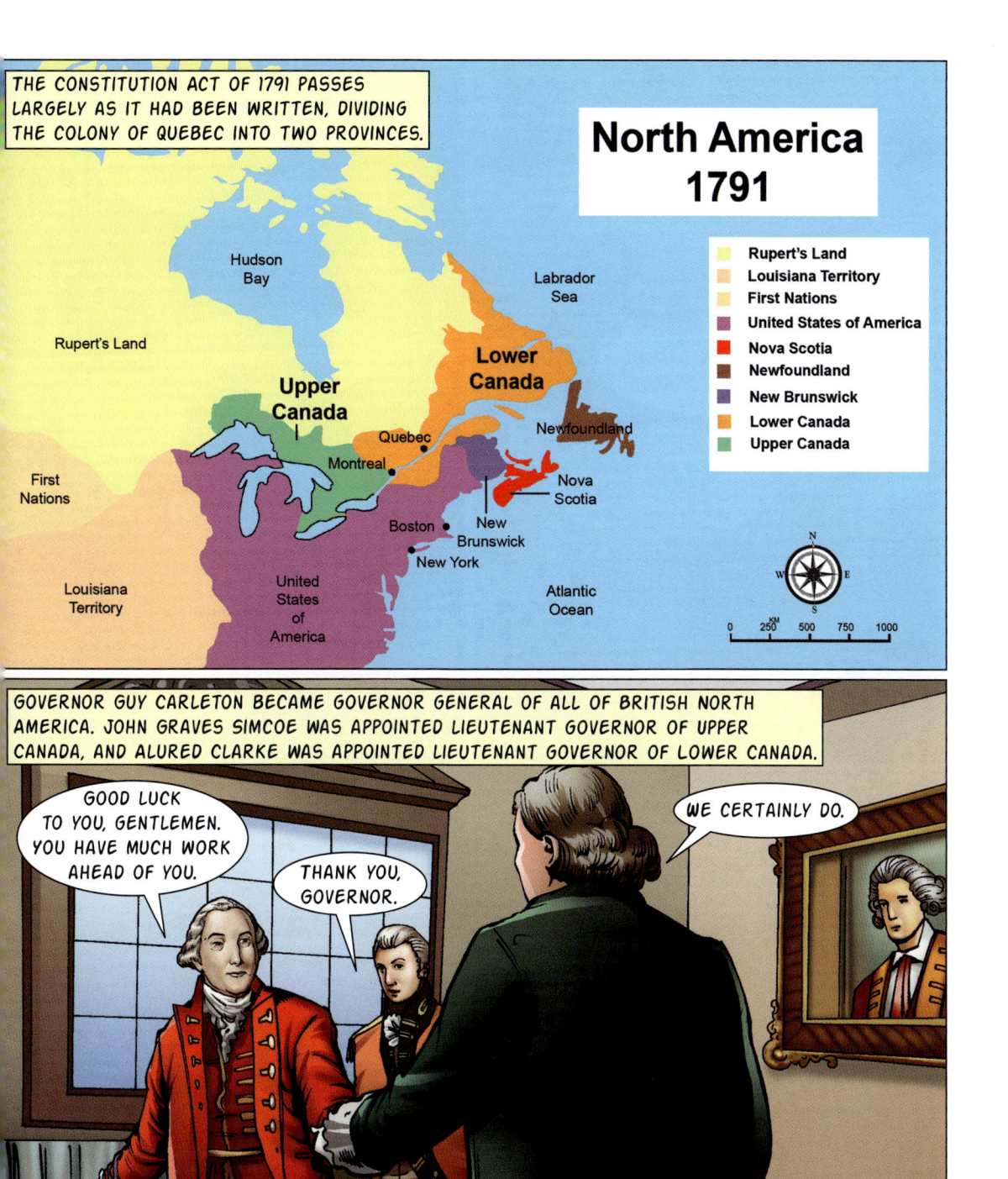

THE CONSTITUTION ACT OF 1791 PASSES LARGELY AS IT HAD BEEN WRITTEN, DIVIDING THE COLONY OF QUEBEC INTO TWO PROVINCES.

North America 1791

- Rupert's Land
- Louisiana Territory
- First Nations
- United States of America
- Nova Scotia
- Newfoundland
- New Brunswick
- Lower Canada
- Upper Canada

GOVERNOR GUY CARLETON BECAME GOVERNOR GENERAL OF ALL OF BRITISH NORTH AMERICA. JOHN GRAVES SIMCOE WAS APPOINTED LIEUTENANT GOVERNOR OF UPPER CANADA, AND ALURED CLARKE WAS APPOINTED LIEUTENANT GOVERNOR OF LOWER CANADA.

"GOOD LUCK TO YOU, GENTLEMEN. YOU HAVE MUCH WORK AHEAD OF YOU."

"THANK YOU, GOVERNOR."

"WE CERTAINLY DO."

IN UPPER CANADA...
YOU, SIRS, HAVE BEEN APPOINTED BY THE CROWN. YOU WILL SERVE AS MY LEGISLATIVE COUNCIL.
WE WILL MAINTAIN ORDER IN UPPER CANADA.
WE WILL ALSO RESTRAIN ANY UNRULY TENDENCIES OF DEMOCRACY.
YOU, SIRS, HAVE BEEN ELECTED TO SERVE THE PEOPLE OF UPPER CANADA.
YES, AT THE LEISURE OF THE UPPER HOUSE.
WE HAVE NO REAL POWER.
CITIZENS WERE SUBJECT TO BRITISH CRIMINAL, CIVIL, AND PROPERTY LAWS.
FINALLY, WE HAVE ACCESS TO THE LAND. WE CAN BUILD NEW HOMES AND FARMS.
YES, BUT I HEAR THERE WILL BE MORE TAXES TO PAY.
ONE IN EVERY SEVEN ACRES WAS RESERVED FOR THE CHURCH OF ENGLAND.
OUR NEW CHURCH IS ALMOST FINISHED. YOU MAY USE OUR GROUND FOR YOUR STUDENTS UNTIL THE SCHOOL IS BUILT.
THANK YOU. I'M SO GRATEFUL THAT PROPERTY HAS BEEN SET ASIDE FOR SCHOOLS AS WELL.

IN LOWER CANADA...
WE HAVE THE SAME GOVERNMENT STRUCTURE AS OUR NEIGHBORS IN UPPER CANADA.
WE ARE ELECTED TO MAKE THE LAWS FOR UPPER CANADA.
YES, BUT THOSE LAWS ARE SUBJECT TO APPROVAL BY THE UPPER HOUSE AND THE LIEUTENANT GOVERNOR.
WE HOLD THE REAL POWER.
COLONISTS WERE STILL REQUIRED TO PAY TITHES, OR LAND TAXES, TO THE ROMAN CATHOLIC CHURCH.
AT LEAST THOSE OF US WHO OWN THE LAND CAN VOTE AND HOLD OFFICE NOW.
YES, AND YOU CAN ATTEND THE CATHOLIC CHURCH AND SPEAK FRENCH FREELY.
THE COLONY WAS OFFICIALLY DIVIDED. DIFFERENCES SIMMERED BETWEEN THE FRENCH AND THE BRITISH, AS WELL AS AMONG THE WEALTHY LANDHOLDERS WHO DOMINATED GOVERNMENT AND THE REST OF THE COLONISTS.
THIS ISN'T WORKING.
ÇA NE MARCHE PAS.

IN 1812, THE UNITED STATES DECLARED WAR ON GREAT BRITAIN OVER TRADE CONFLICTS. THE WAR TEMPORARILY UNITED LOWER AND UPPER CANADA IN SUPPORT OF GREAT BRITAIN. AFTER THE WAR, HOWEVER, THE POLITICAL AND ECONOMIC CONFLICTS IN CANADA BECAME MORE PRONOUNCED.
OLIGARCHIES OF WEALTHY LANDHOLDERS, MERCHANTS, AND BANKERS DOMINATED BOTH UPPER AND LOWER CANADA.
THE FAMILY COMPACT RULE UPPER CANADA LIKE KINGS.
THEY HAVE CREATED A CLASS SOCIETY JUST LIKE IN GREAT BRITAIN.
THE COMPACT CONTROLS THE LAND AND COLLECTS RENTS TO LINE THEIR OWN POCKETS.
THE CHÂTEAU CLIQUE, THEY HORDE THE WEALTH AND POWER OF LOWER CANADA.
THEY USE ALL THE TAX MONEY WE PAY TO FURTHER THEIR OWN BUSINESS.
THE ENGLISH STILL RULE US. THEY DENY OUR FRENCH ASSEMBLY THE POWER TO GOVERN.

THE DISCONTENT AMONG BRITISH AND FRENCH COLONISTS LED TO REBELLION. NEWSPAPER PUBLISHER WILLIAM LYON MACKENZIE ORGANIZED DISSENT IN UPPER CANADA. LANDHOLDER LOUIS-JOSEPH PAPINEAU, LEADER OF THE PARTI PATRIOTE IN THE ASSEMBLY, RALLIED REBELS IN LOWER CANADA.
THE ANGLICAN CHURCH AND LAND SPECULATORS HOLD TOO MUCH POWER. WE MUST RETAKE OUR GOVERNMENT!
THE ENGLISH HAVE ALREADY DRIVEN UP THE COST OF OUR LANDS. THEY ARE RUINING OUR WAY OF LIFE. WHAT WILL THEY DO NEXT?
PAPINEU INDEPENDENCE
REBELLION IS BREWING IN BOTH LOWER AND UPPER CANADA. PAPINEAU HAS CALLED THE REBELS TO ARMS.
HE IS A TRAITOR. ARREST HIM!

ON OCTOBER 24, 1837, PAPINEAU SPOKE TO A CROWD OF MORE THAN 5,000 COLONISTS AT SAINT-CHARLES. SOME PATRIOTES, INCLUDING WOLFRED NELSON, DID NOT THINK THAT PAPINEAU WAS MOVING FAST ENOUGH.
ASSEMBLE NOW!...ELECT YOUR OWN JUSTICES OF THE PEACE. TAKE BACK THE GOVERNMENT!
THE TIME FOR WORDS IS DONE. I BELIEVE THAT THE MOMENT HAS COME TO MELT DOWN OUR TIN PLATES AND TIN SPOONS AND FORGE THEM INTO BULLETS.
THE NEXT MONTH, BATTLE ERUPTED BETWEEN BRITISH FORCES AND THE PATRIOTES, LED BY WOLFRED NELSON.
VICTORY!
THE PATRIOTES OF LOWER CANADA PREVAILED IN THEIR FIRST BATTLE WITH THE BRITISH. HOWEVER, THE BRITISH FOUGHT BACK AND DEFEATED THE REBELS AT SAINT-CHARLES AND SAINT-EUSTACHE.
THE BRITISH ARE TOO STRONG HERE. WE MUST FLEE TO THE UNITED STATES.
WE MUST REGROUP.

MEANWHILE, IN UPPER CANADA, WILLIAM LYON MACKENZIE ORGANIZED REBELS AT MONTGOMERY'S TAVERN IN TORONTO TO PROTEST THE RULE OF THE COLONIAL GOVERNMENT. ON DECEMBER 7, MACKENZIE LED HUNDREDS OF PROTESTORS IN A MARCH.

THE MILITIA HAS BLOCKED YONGE STREET.

YOU MUST DISPERSE, OR WE WILL FIRE!

LIKE PAPINEAU AND NELSON, MACKENZIE WAS FORCED TO FLEE TO THE UNITED STATES WHEN HIS FORCES WERE ROUTED OUTSIDE TORONTO. FOR MONTHS, REBELS FROM UPPER AND LOWER CANADA MADE PLANS AND CONDUCTED SKIRMISHES ACROSS THE BORDER FROM THE UNITED STATES INTO CANADA.

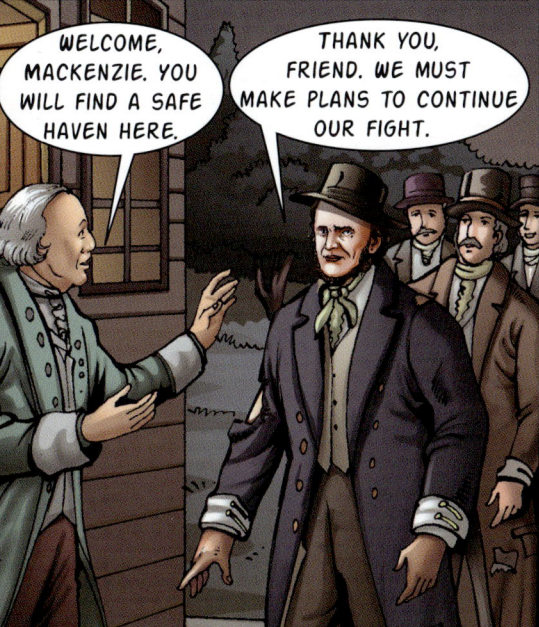

WELCOME, MACKENZIE. YOU WILL FIND A SAFE HAVEN HERE.

THANK YOU, FRIEND. WE MUST MAKE PLANS TO CONTINUE OUR FIGHT.

THE GOVERNOR, LORD GOSFORD, RESPONDED BY SUSPENDING THE CONSTITUTION AND TIGHTENING CONTROL OF LOWER AND UPPER CANADA.

MARTIAL LAW HAS BEEN DECLARED. THE REBELS ARE TRAITORS TO THE CROWN!

SKIRMISHES FROM ACROSS THE BORDER CONTINUED INTO 1838, BUT THE REBELS NEVER SUCCEEDED IN WRESTING CONTROL FROM THE BRITISH IN UPPER OR LOWER CANADA. STILL, THE REBELLION CAUSED GREAT CONCERN AMONG BRITISH LEADERS IN PARLIAMENT.
I AM JOHN GEORGE LAMBTON, EARL OF DURHAM. I HAVE BEEN SENT HERE TO RESOLVE THE CANADIAN QUESTION.
WELCOME, LORD DURHAM!
IN 1839, LORD DURHAM WROTE AND SUBMITTED HIS *REPORT ON THE AFFAIRS OF BRITISH NORTH AMERICA*, COMMONLY KNOWN AS THE DURHAM REPORT.
CANADA CANNOT CONTINUE DIVIDED. WE CANNOT YET UNITE ALL THE BRITISH COLONIES, BUT WE MUST UNITE UPPER AND LOWER CANADA AND INSTITUTE A RESPONSIBLE GOVERNMENT.
PARLIAMENT REVIEWED THE DURHAM REPORT AND MOVED TO PASS THE ACT OF UNION IN 1840. THIS LAW IMPLEMENTED SOME, BUT NOT ALL, OF DURHAM'S RECOMMENDATIONS.
WHAT DOES HE MEAN "RESPONSIBLE GOVERNMENT"?
DURHAM WANTS TO GIVE MORE POWER TO THE VOTERS. THEY WILL ELECT REPRESENTATIVES TO AN ASSEMBLY, FROM WHICH THE EXECUTIVE WILL BE CHOSEN.
ABSURD! THAT'S TOO MUCH POWER TO THE COLONISTS. IT WILL LEAD TO CHAOS.
HOW CAN THIS BE CALLED RESPONSIBLE?
THE ACT OF UNION UNITED UPPER AND LOWER CANADA INTO THE UNITED PROVINCE OF CANADA UNDER A GOVERNOR GENERAL APPOINTED BY BRITISH PARLIAMENT. CHARLES POULETT THOMSON SERVED AS THE FIRST GOVERNOR GENERAL OF THE UNITED COLONY.
UPPER CANADA WILL NOW BE KNOWN AS CANADA WEST, AND LOWER CANADA WILL NOW BE KNOWN AS CANADA EAST. WE WILL HAVE ONE UNITED GOVERNMENT TO REPRESENT BOTH. DO YOU CONSENT?
WE CONSENT!

ALTHOUGH THE ACT OF UNION UNITED THE TWO CANADAS UNDER ONE GOVERNMENT WITH AN ELECTED ASSEMBLY, IT DID NOT CREATE RESPONSIBLE GOVERNMENT. THE EXECUTIVE STILL ANSWERED TO THE BRITISH PARLIAMENT, NOT THE COLONISTS.

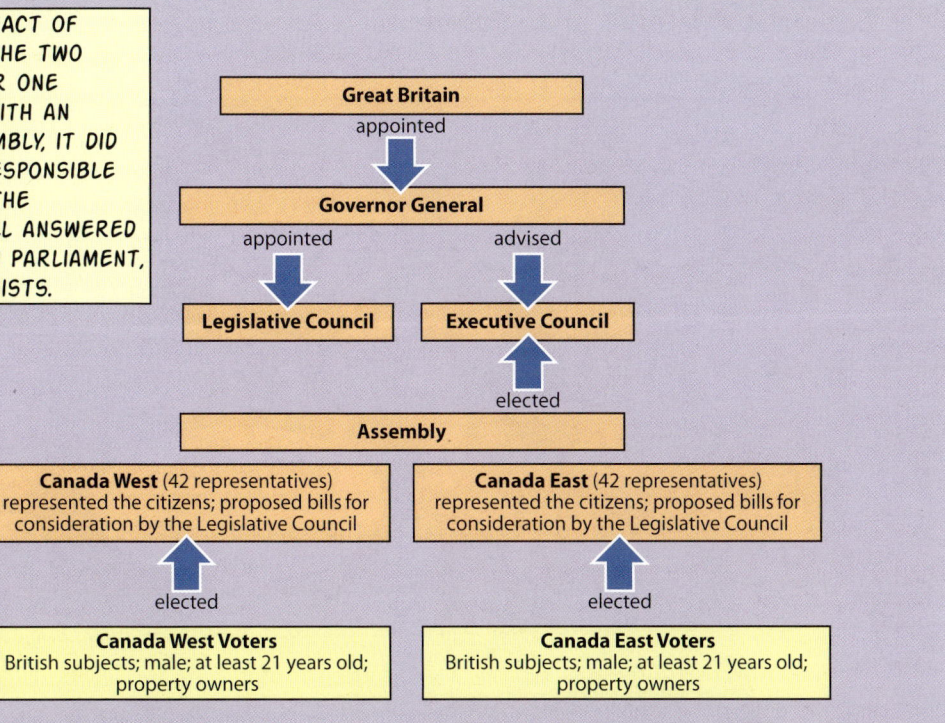

Great Britain
appointed ↓

Governor General
appointed ↓   advised ↓

Legislative Council   **Executive Council**
↑ elected

Assembly

Canada West (42 representatives) represented the citizens; proposed bills for consideration by the Legislative Council

Canada East (42 representatives) represented the citizens; proposed bills for consideration by the Legislative Council

↑ elected   ↑ elected

Canada West Voters
British subjects; male; at least 21 years old; property owners

Canada East Voters
British subjects; male; at least 21 years old; property owners

---

THE PUSH FOR RESPONSIBLE GOVERNMENT HAD BEGUN. CANADIAN POLITICIANS LOUIS-HIPPOLYTE LAFONTAINE AND ROBERT BALDWIN LED REFORM-MINDED LEADERS TO ORGANIZE THE UNITED REFORM PARTY.

"THE FRENCH OUTNUMBER THE BRITISH, AND YET WE HAVE THE SAME NUMBER OF SEATS."

"WE MUST WORK TOGETHER, BRITISH AND FRENCH REFORMERS. TOGETHER, WE CAN CHANGE THE GOVERNMENT."

THE **INDUSTRIAL REVOLUTION** STIMULATED GROWTH IN BUSINESS AND TRADE. THE INCREASE IN ECONOMIC ACTIVITY ENCOURAGED THE BRITISH GOVERNMENT TO GRANT THE COLONIES GREATER ECONOMIC AND POLITICAL FREEDOM.
DID YOU HEAR? THE TARIFFS ON GRAIN HAVE FINALLY BEEN REPEALED.
YES, AND THE REFORMERS ARE GAINING SEATS IN THE ASSEMBLY. CHANGE IS COMING.

IN 1848, THE BRITISH GOVERNMENT, LED BY THE PRIME MINISTER, LORD JOHN RUSSELL, BEGAN GRANTING RESPONSIBLE GOVERNMENT TO ITS NORTH AMERICAN COLONIES.
THE COLONIAL GOVERNMENTS SHOULD HONOR THE WILL OF THEIR ELECTED ASSEMBLIES.

THE FOLLOWING YEAR, THE REFORM ASSEMBLY OF LAFONTAINE AND BALDWIN PASSED A LAW COMPENSATING VICTIMS OF THE 1837 AND 1838 REBELLIONS AND GRANTED AMNESTY TO THE REBELS. GOVERNOR GENERAL JAMES BRUCE, KNOWN AS LORD ELGIN, SIGNED THE LAW.
NOT ALL WILL LIKE IT, BUT IT IS WHAT THE ASSEMBLY DECIDED.
FINALLY, THE GOVERNMENT REFLECTS THE WILL OF THE VOTERS.
YES, WE HAVE A GOVERNMENT RESPONSIBLE TO THE PEOPLE.

THE COLONIES OF CANADA WERE NOT CONTENT WITH RESPONSIBLE GOVERNMENT. IN 1863, GEORGE BROWN AND JOHN A. MACDONALD OF CANADA WEST MET WITH GEORGE ÉTIENNE CARTIER OF CANADA EAST AND FORMED THE GREAT COALITION.
OUR PARTIES, WORKING TOGETHER, HAVE PREVENTED DEADLOCK IN THE PROVINCE OF CANADA.
YES, AND NOW WE MUST CONVINCE THE MARITIMES TO JOIN US.
THE FOLLOWING YEAR, PROMINENT LEADERS OF THE THREE MARITIME PROVINCES DECIDED TO PUSH FURTHER FOR SELF-GOVERNMENT.
IT MAKES SENSE FOR NOVA SCOTIA, PRINCE EDWARD ISLAND, AND NEW BRUNSWICK TO FORM A MARITIME UNION.
IT IS TIME THE MARITIMES HAD GREATER INDEPENDENCE.
IT IS TIME FOR ALL CANADA TO PURSUE THAT GOAL.
WE URGE YOU TO UNITE AND FORM A UNION WITH THE PROVINCE OF CANADA.
I AM NOT CONVINCED THAT A WIDER UNION WOULD BENEFIT US.
AT FIRST, PRINCE EDWARD ISLAND RESISTED THE UNION. IN 1866, DELEGATES FROM CANADA, NOVA SCOTIA, AND NEW BRUNSWICK MET AT THE LONDON CONFERENCE.
WE HAVE REACHED AN AGREEMENT.
OUR PROVINCES WILL BE UNITED AS THE NEW DOMINION OF CANADA.
IT WILL BE THE FIRST DOMINION IN THE BRITISH EMPIRE.

IN 1867, THE AGREEMENT PASSED PARLIAMENT AS THE BRITISH NORTH AMERICA ACT. QUEEN VICTORIA APPROVED THE LAW. ON JULY 1, THE DOMINION OF CANADA WAS OFFICIALLY DECLARED.
BY THE QUEEN!
A PROCLAMATION
For Uniting the Provinces of Canada, Nova Scotia, and New Brunswick, into one Dominion, under the name of CANADA.
VICTORIA R.
GOD SAVE THE QUEEN.
THE DOMINION OF CANADA COMPRISED NOT THREE BUT FOUR PROVINCES. OTHER PROVINCES WOULD JOIN IN LATER YEARS, INCLUDING PRINCE EDWARD ISLAND IN 1873. JOHN A. MACDONALD WAS APPOINTED THE FIRST PRIME MINISTER OF CANADA.
OUR NEW CONFEDERATION WILL BE GOVERNED BY A CONSTITUTION SIMILAR IN PRINCIPLE TO THAT OF THE UNITED KINGDOM.
SO WE'RE STILL PART OF GREAT BRITAIN?
YES, BUT WE HAVE OUR OWN LAWS AND GOVERNMENT, ANSWERABLE TO OUR OWN VOTERS.
THE PROVINCES HAVE SOME SPECIFIC POWERS, BUT THEY'RE STILL SUBJECT TO THE CENTRAL GOVERNMENT.
THE FRENCH WILL KEEP THEIR LANGUAGE.

THE NEW GOVERNMENT DIVIDED LEGISLATIVE POWER BETWEEN AN APPOINTED SENATE AND AN ELECTED HOUSE OF COMMONS. QUEEN VICTORIA AND THE BRITISH CROWN RETAINED EXECUTIVE POWER. THE LAW ALSO PROVIDED FOR A SUPREME COURT AND PROVINCIAL COURT SYSTEMS WITH APPOINTED JUDGES.

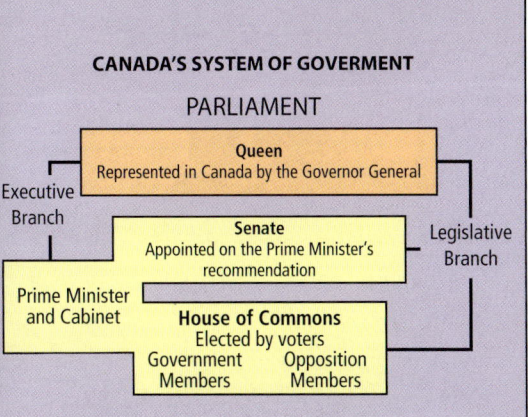

CANADA'S SYSTEM OF GOVERMENT

PARLIAMENT

- **Queen** — Represented in Canada by the Governor General
- **Senate** — Appointed on the Prime Minister's recommendation
- **House of Commons** — Elected by voters (Government Members / Opposition Members)

Executive Branch: Prime Minister and Cabinet
Legislative Branch

"I AM STILL YOUR **SOVEREIGN**, PRIME MINISTER."

"YES, YOUR MAJESTY, BUT CANADA HAS FINALLY ACHIEVED SOME INDEPENDENCE. SURELY, YOU WON'T BE OVERLY BOTHERED BY OUR AFFAIRS."

"THE COURTS WILL JUDGE MATTERS OF THE LAW AS WE ALWAYS HAVE. THE FEDERAL GOVERNMENT SETS OUR CRIMINAL LAWS."

"YES, BUT THE PROVINCES DETERMINE CIVIL LAW."

CANADIAN LEADERS QUICKLY TURNED THEIR ATTENTION WEST, TOWARD THE VAST AMOUNT OF LAND BETWEEN ONTARIO AND THE PACIFIC OCEAN. UNDER PRIME MINISTER MACDONALD, THE DOMINION ACQUIRED NEW LANDS.

WHERE ARE YOU ALL GOING?

HAVEN'T YOU HEARD? THE DOMINION'S GAINED TWO NEW PROVINCES, BRITISH COLUMBIA AND MANITOBA.

WE'RE GOING TO BE SETTLERS OUT WEST!

THE BRITISH GOVERNMENT HAD SECURED THE LOYALTY OF ABORIGINAL PEOPLES WITH THE PROCLAMATION OF 1763. HOWEVER, RENEWED DEMANDS FOR WESTERN LANDS LED CANADIAN OFFICIALS TO NEGOTIATE NEW TREATIES BETWEEN 1871 AND 1877.

IF YOU MOVE TO THE RESERVES, WE WILL GIVE YOU SCHOOLS, MEDICINES, AND OTHER HELP.

IN RETURN, YOU MUST RENOUNCE CLAIM TO THE REST OF YOUR LANDS.

YOU KNOW HOW OUR BRETHREN IN THE UNITED STATES HAVE SUFFERED. WHAT CHOICE DO WE HAVE?

FOR THE SAKE OF OUR PEOPLE AND THEIR SURVIVAL, WE WILL AGREE.

IN 1885, THE TRANSCONTINENTAL RAILROAD ACROSS CANADA WAS COMPLETED. THE RAILROAD, POPULATION GROWTH, AND POLITICAL AND ECONOMIC AMBITION COMBINED TO CREATE AN EVEN LARGER CANADA BY THE TURN OF THE CENTURY.

WE JOINED IN 1871.

WE JOINED THE DOMINION IN 1870.

AND WE FINALLY JOINED IN 1905.

26

THE 1867 BRITISH NORTH AMERICAN ACT SERVED AS CANADA'S CONSTITUTION FOR MORE THAN 100 YEARS. NEWFOUNDLAND BECAME CANADA'S TENTH PROVINCE IN 1949, AND IN JANUARY 1965, QUEEN ELIZABETH PROCLAIMED...
TODAY, CANADA HAS ITS OWN FLAG.
AS CANADA GREW, THE GOVERNMENT ENCOUNTERED PROBLEMS WITH ITS OWN STRUCTURE.
IN THE PAST CENTURY, WE HAVE AMENDED THE CONSTITUTION 20 TIMES.
YES, AND EACH TIME, WE'VE HAD TO SEEK THE PERMISSION OF THE BRITISH PARLIAMENT.
IT IS AN UNNECESSARY BURDEN. WE ARE OUR OWN COUNTRY.
NOT EXACTLY.
IN 1980, CANADIAN PRIME MINISTER PIERRE TRUDEAU MADE A BOLD MOVE. HE ANNOUNCED THAT HIS GOVERNMENT WOULD TAKE STEPS TO PATRIATE AND REFORM THE CANADIAN CONSTITUTION.
IT IS TIME THAT CANADA BECOME TRULY SOVEREIGN! IT IS TIME TO BRING THE CONSTITUTION, OUR LAWS, OUR GOVERNMENT, HOME.

CITIZENS OF QUEBEC HAD ALSO BEGUN TO DEMAND THEIR OWN NATION. RENÉ LÉVESQUE, QUEBEC'S PREMIER, CALLED FOR QUEBEC'S INDEPENDENCE.

"WE HAVE OUR OWN LANGUAGE AND CULTURE. WE SHOULD HAVE OUR OWN COUNTRY."

REFERENDUM RESULTS
59.5% NO

ON MAY 20, 1980, CITIZENS OF QUEBEC WENT TO THE POLLS TO VOTE ON THE ISSUE OF SEPARATION.

PRIME MINISTER TRUDEAU MET WITH PROVINCIAL LEADERS MANY TIMES TO SECURE **PATRIATION** OF THE CANADIAN CONSTITUTION, BUT GOVERNMENT LEADERS FAILED TO AGREE ON THE AMENDMENT PROCESS.

"THE MAJORITY OF THE PROVINCES WILL NOT CONSENT TO A PATRIATION BILL THAT GIVES SO MUCH POWER TO THE FEDERAL GOVERNMENT."

WHEN TRUDEAU THREATENED TO GO TO THE BRITISH PARLIAMENT AND PATRIATE THE CONSTITUTION WITHOUT PROVINCIAL ACCORD, PROVINCIAL PREMIERS APPEALED TO CANADA'S SUPREME COURT.

"THE PRIME MINISTER MAY NOT REQUIRE OUR CONSENT FOR PATRIATION, BUT WITHOUT IT, HE VIOLATES OUR CONSTITUTIONAL CONVENTIONS."

IN NOVEMBER 1981, JEAN CHRÉTIEN MET WITH SEVERAL PREMIERS IN OTTAWA. AT THE END OF THE NIGHT, THEY HAD REACHED AN AGREEMENT ON PATRIATION AND INDEPENDENCE.

"FINALLY."

"OUR KITCHEN ACCORD IS DONE."

"WILL TRUDEAU AND THE OTHER PREMIERS ACCEPT IT?"

TRUDEAU AND NINE PROVINCIAL PREMIERS APPROVED THE KITCHEN ACCORD. QUEBEC REFUSED.

"WE BETTER GRAB THE SIGNATURES, THIS PAPER, AND RUN BEFORE ANYONE CHANGES HIS MIND!"

"THIS NEW CONSTITUTION IS A THREAT TO FRENCH CANADA'S CULTURAL SURVIVAL."

ON APRIL 17, 1982, QUEEN ELIZABETH II SIGNED THE CONSTITUTION ACT.

"THE DOMINION OF CANADA IS NOW AN INDEPENDENT NATION."

"CANADA'S CONSTITUTION HAS COME HOME!"

- Retained provisions of the British North America Act (renamed the Constitution Act of 1867)
- Provided a Charter of Rights and Freedoms for all citizens
- Introduced a process for constitutional amendment

CANADA HAD ITS OWN CONSTITUTION, BUT NEGOTIATIONS CONTINUED. IN 1987, THE PROVINCIAL PREMIERS MET WITH QUEBEC'S PREMIER ROBERT BOURASSA TO SECURE QUEBEC'S PARTICIPATION.

"QUEBEC MUST BE RECOGNIZED AS A **DISTINCT SOCIETY**. CANADA MUST BE CONFIRMED AS A BILINGUAL NATION."

"AGREED, AND ALL PROVINCES MUST AGREE TO CHANGES IN OUR CENTRAL INSTITUTIONS."

ALL PROVINCES HAD TO AGREE TO THE MEECH LAKE ACCORD, BUT NEWFOUNDLAND AND MANITOBA FAILED TO APPROVE IT BY THE 1990 DEADLINE. IN MANITOBA, ELIJAH HARPER WORKED TO PREVENT PASSAGE OF THE ACCORD.

"IT IS TIME TO RESPECT THE RIGHTS OF OUR ABORIGINAL PEOPLES."

IN JULY 1992, JOE CLARK CONVENED A NEW MEETING. REPRESENTATIVES FROM ABORIGINAL NATIONS, INCLUDING OVIDE MERCREDI, AND PROVINCIAL PREMIERS, EXCEPT FOR QUEBEC, ATTENDED.

"THIS ACCORD RETAINS MUCH OF THE MEECH LAKE ACCORD, AND IT PROVIDES FOR ABORIGINAL SELF-GOVERNMENT."

"FINALLY, RECOGNITION FOR ABORIGINAL PEOPLES."

MANY CANADIANS FELT THIS NEW CHARLOTTETOWN ACCORD WAS TOO VAGUE, BUT IN OCTOBER 1992, IT WAS PUT UP FOR VOTE.

"WITH THE ACCORD DEFEATED, WHAT DO YOU THINK WILL HAPPEN NEXT?"

TO THIS DAY, QUEBEC REMAINS SYMBOLICALLY OUTSIDE THE CONSTITUTIONAL FOLD.

Brain Teasers

1. When Great Britain took control of New France in 1763, what major problem did Governor Murray face?
2. Why did Governor Carleton try to appease French landholders and clergy?
3. What impact did the migration of British Loyalists from the United States of America to Quebec have?
4. What were the major provisions of the Constitution Act of 1791?
5. Why did many Canadians resent the Family Compact and the Château Clique?
6. What did William Lyon Mackenzie and Louis-Joseph Papineau hope to achieve with their rebellions in 1837 and 1838?
7. What document served as the first constitution of the Dominion of Canada?
8. What major change did the Constitution Act of 1982 enact for Canada?

Answers

1. The population of New France was mostly French colonists, who were Roman Catholics. They were not eligible to participate in the government.
2. Carleton believed that the colony had to be governed by its people. He also believed that Great Britain would need Quebec's help because the American colonies were about to revolt.
3. British Loyalists demanded more British customs and representation in an assembly.
4. The act split Quebec into two colonial provinces. Lower Canada would remain predominantly French; Upper Canada would be mostly British. Each province would have its own lieutenant governor, executive and legislative councils, and elected assembly. These governments would remain subject to a governor general appointed by the British Parliament.
5. They were ruling oligarchies of wealthy landholders, bankers, and merchants who controlled the government of Upper and Lower Canada and used tax monies for their own advancement.
6. The two men wanted more responsible democracy for Upper and Lower Canada.
7. The British North America Act of 1867 (later renamed the Constitution Act of 1867) served as the first constitution.
8. With the Constitution Act of 1982, the Dominion of Canada became a sovereign nation, independent of Great Britain.

Further Information

How can I find out more about the Canadian Constitution?

Most libraries have computers that connect to a database that contains information on books and articles about different subjects. You can input a key word and find material on the person, place, or thing you want to learn more about. The computer will provide you with a list of books in the library that contain information on the subject you searched for. Non-fiction books are arranged numerically, using their call numbers. Fiction books are organized alphabetically by the author's last name.

Books

McTeer, Maureen. *Parliament: Canada's Democracy and How It Works*. Random House of Canada, 1995.

Milne, David. *The Canadian Constitution: The Players in the Process that Led from Patriation to Meech Lake to an Uncertain Future*. Lorimer, 1991.

Webber, Jeremy. *Reimagining Canada: Language, Culture, Community, and the Canadian Constitution*. McGill-Queen's University Press, 1994.

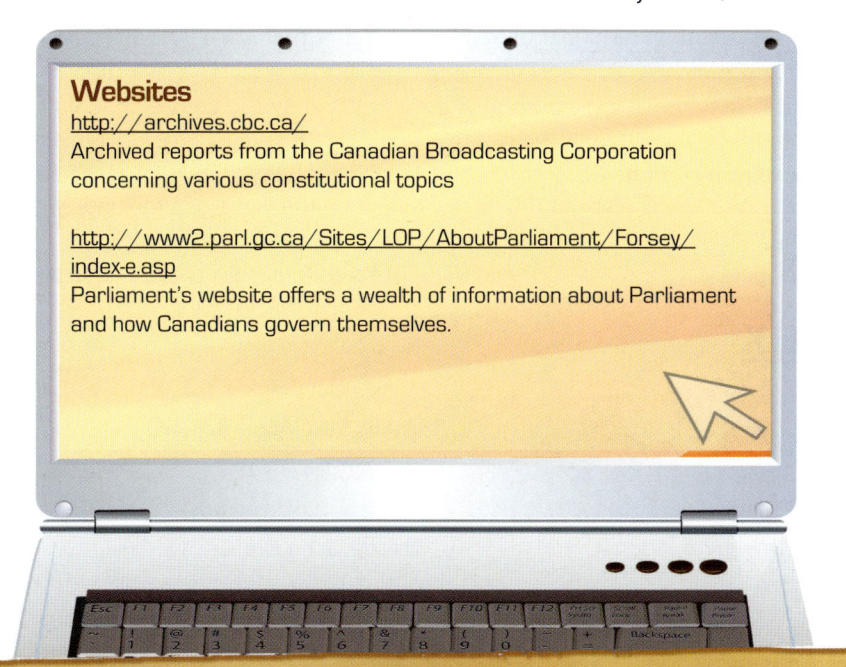

Websites

http://archives.cbc.ca/
Archived reports from the Canadian Broadcasting Corporation concerning various constitutional topics

http://www2.parl.gc.ca/Sites/LOP/AboutParliament/Forsey/index-e.asp
Parliament's website offers a wealth of information about Parliament and how Canadians govern themselves.

Glossary

assimilate: to absorb, or blend into, the customs of a particular population or group of people

civil law: rules and cases that deal with the rights of private citizens, such as disputes over contracts, property ownership, divorce, and child custody

criminal law: rules and cases that pertain to actions that are prohibited by the government because they threaten or harm public safety and welfare

democracy: a system of government in which people hold the power and choose their leaders and participate in making laws through a free election process

distinct society: denoting the uniqueness of Quebec within Canada

Industrial Revolution: a period in history beginning in the mid-1700s, when power-driven machines were first used to manufacture and produce goods in large quantities

Loyalists: American colonists who were loyal to the government of Great Britain

Meech Lake Accord: a constitutional agreement that would have recognized the distinctiveness of Quebec in the Canadian Confederation and granted an enhanced role for the provinces in their relationships with the federal government

oligarchies: systems of government in which a small number of people hold the power

patriation: the act of taking over the power to amend the Canadian Constitution from the British Parliament; turning over legislative powers that were formerly held by the mother country

representative democracy: a system of government in which people elect leaders who make laws and represent the voters

responsible government: government responsible to the representatives of the people, an executive, or Cabinet that is dependent on the votes of a majority in the elected legislature

sovereign: person who holds supreme authority; freedom from outside control

Index

Aboriginal Peoples 4, 6, 26, 29
Carleton, Guy 4, 7, 8, 10, 13
Charlottetown Accord 29
Durham Report 4, 20
Grenville, William 4, 11, 12
Harper, Elijah 4, 29
Lambton, John George 4, 20
Mackenzie, William 17, 19
Meech Lake Accord 4, 29
Murray, James 6, 7
Papineau, Louis-Joseph 17, 18, 19
Simcoe, John Graves 13, 14
Trudeau, Pierre 4, 27, 28, 29

DATE DUE

APR 0 4 2017

Return Material Promptly